Creative Juices Publishing

Made in the USA
Coppell, TX
11 November 2020

41114067R10061